cat
แมว
maeo

rabbit

กระต่าย

kratai

dog

สุนัข

sunak

chick

ลูกไก่
lukkai

duck
เป็ด
pet

sheep

แกะ

kae

goat
แพะ
phae

pig

หมู

mu

donkey

ลา

la

horse

ม้า

ma

cow

วัว

wua

mouse

หนู

nu

bat

ค้างคาว

khangkhao

bee

ผึ้ง

phueng

spider

แมงมุม

maengmum

fox

สุนัขจิ้งจอก

sunakchingchok

deer

กวาง

kwang

squirrel

กระรอก

krarok

hedgehog

เม่น

men

owl

นกฮูก

nokhuk

frog

กบ

kop

snake

ງູ

ngu

racoon

แรคคูน

rae

parrot

นกแก้ว

nokkaeo

toucan

นกทูแคน
nok thu khaen

alligator

จระเข้

chorakhe

sea turtle

เต่าทะเล

taothale

flamingo

นกฟลามิงโก้

nok fla ming ko

penguin

เพนกวิน

phenkawin

crab

ปู

pu

jellyfish

แมงกะพรุน

maengkaphrun

seal

แมวน้ำ

maeonam

shark

ปลาฉลาม

plachalam

whale

วาฬ

wan

orca

วาฬเพชฌฆาต

wanphetchakhat

starfish
ปลาดาว
pladao

rhinoceros

แรด

raet

panda

หมีแพนด้า

miphaenda

monkey

ลิง

ling

lion

สิงโต

singto

tiger

เสือ

suea

elephant

ช้าง

chang